CROCODILIANS

by Joan Short and Bettina Bird

Illustrated by Deborah Savin

This edition first published in the United States in 1997 by
MONDO Publishing
By arrangement with MULTIMEDIA INTERNATIONAL (UK) LTD

The publisher would like to thank Peter Brazaitis, Curator of Animals, Central Park Wildlife Center, New York City; Dr. Stephen Garnett; Professor F. W. King, Florida State Museum; Dr. Kent A. Vliet, University of Florida; Mr. Neil Mackenzie; Dr. George Vorlicek, University of Sydney; and Dr. Grahame Webb, Northern Territory Conservation Commission, Australia, for their assistance in the preparation of this book.

Photograph Credits: Frans Lanting/Tony Stone Images: front cover; Ian Morris: pp. 4, 24, 26, 28; Bill Green: pp. 7 left, 9 left, 10, 23; Jack Green: pp. 7 right, 8, 20, 21, 22, 27, 33, 34, 35, 41, 45; Dr. Grahame Webb: pp. 9 right, 16, 17, 18 left, 29, 40, 43, 44; D.G. Anderson/National Photo Index of Australian Wildlife: p. 18 right; Peter Farkas: p. 25; John B. Thorbjarnarson/Florida State Museum: pp. 31 left, 32; Dr. Kent A. Vliet/University of Florida: p. 31 right; Pavel German/A.N.T. Photo Library: p. 38; Dr. Tirtha Maskey/University of Florida: pp. 39, 46; State Reference Library of the Northern Territory/Northern Australian Collection: p. 42.

Text copyright © 1988 by Joan Short and Bettina Bird
Illustrations copyright © 1988 by Multimedia International (UK) Ltd

For information contact:
MONDO Publishing
980 Avenue of the Americas
New York, NY 10018
Visit our website at www.mondopub.com

Printed in China
First Mondo printing, January 1997
09 10 11   10 9 8 7 6 5

Originally published in Australia in 1988 by Horwitz Publications Pty Ltd
Original development by Robert Andersen & Associates and Snowball Educational
Designed by Deborah Savin   Cover redesign by Charlotte Staub

Library of Congress Cataloging-in-Publication Data
Short, Joan.
    Crocodilians / by Joan Short and Bettina Bird ; illustrated by Deborah Savin.
        p.   cm. — (Mondo animals)
    "Originally published in Australia in 1988 by Horwitz Publications"—T.p. verso
    Includes index.
    Summary: Describes the features, habitats, and conservation of crocodiles, alligators, and gharials.
    ISBN 1-57255-217-4 (pbk.)
    1.Crocodilia—Juvenile literature. [1. Crocodilia. 2. Crocodiles. 3. Alligators.] I. Bird, Bettina. II. Savin, Deborah, ill. III. Title. IV. Series.
    QL666.C9S54   1997
    597.98—dc20   96-23346
                                                CIP
                                                AC

Cover: Crocodile

CONTENTS

INTRODUCING CROCODILIANS

Crocodilians is the name of the group of large reptiles that consists of crocodiles, alligators (including caimans), and gharials. They live in water and come out on land to bask in the sun and rest.

Crocodilians first appeared in the hot, wet swamplands of Earth about 190 million years ago. In those distant times, reptiles such as the huge dinosaurs dominated Earth. This period of Earth's history is known as the Age of Reptiles.

Fossils of crocodilians that lived during the Age of Reptiles prove that many of them were enormous. The fossil of one crocodilian that inhabited North America 75 million years ago is over 50 feet (15 meters) long and its huge skull has jaws 7 feet (2 meters) long. This is more than twice as large as the skull of any crocodile living today. Scientists have named this fossil crocodile *Phobosuchus*, which means "horror crocodile."

Dinosaurs roamed the Earth for about 100 million years, but they became extinct about 70 million years ago. Crocodilians, however, did not become extinct. Except for their smaller size, today's 23 species of crocodilians are almost exactly like their ancestors.

Appearance

In general, most crocodilians are similar in appearance. A crocodilian has:

◆ a long snout

◆ an elongated body which can be brown, green, black, yellow, or a mixture of these colors

◆ a long, powerful, flat tail

◆ four short legs with webbed, clawed toes on the hind feet

◆ a covering of thick, heavy scales, raised and rugged on the back, mostly smooth on the belly

◆ two eyes on the sides of the head

◆ upper and lower eyelids and a third set of semi-transparent eyelids which move sideways over the eyes to protect them and allow the animal to see underwater

◆ two ears, which are thin slits behind eyes

◆ nostrils on top of the snout

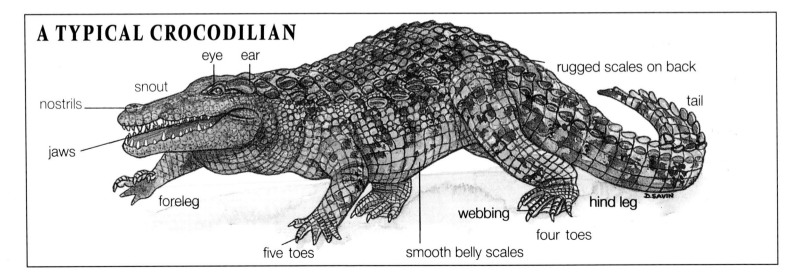

A TYPICAL CROCODILIAN

eye   ear

snout

nostrils

rugged scales on back

tail

jaws

foreleg

hind leg

webbing

four toes

five toes

smooth belly scales

Moving around

When a crocodilian is swimming quickly, its legs lie close to its body while its powerful tail moves from side to side thrusting the body forward, torpedo-like, through the water.

On land, all crocodilians either push their bodies along on their bellies with short, strong legs, or they "high walk" with their legs lifting their bodies off the ground. They use the tough claws on their feet for climbing steep banks and digging.

Crocodilians spend a lot of time floating. The webbing between their toes helps them keep their balance, and their eyes and nostril tips are hardly visible above the surface. When the crocodilian is underwater, its nostrils close and it can hold its breath for about an hour. Tough flaps of leathery skin close over its ears.

◀ **A typical crocodile "high walking"**

▼ **An American alligator so well camouflaged that it is hardly noticeable**

Body temperature

Like all living things, crocodilians will die if they become either too hot or too cold.

Reptiles are "cold-blooded." This means their body temperature is dependent upon the temperature of their surroundings, unlike "warm-blooded" animals such as birds and mammals, including humans, who can regulate their body temperature. Reptiles have to rely on the warmth of the sun, the coolness of water or shady places, or the shelter of dens or burrows to keep their bodies at the right temperature.

A crocodilian spends many hours on land during the day, basking in the sunshine to warm its body. Often it becomes too warm, but it cannot sweat to cool down. Instead, the crocodilian opens its jaws wide when it feels too hot, and the moisture inside its mouth evaporates, helping it to cool off.

A crocodilian usually spends most of the night in water because the water is warmer than land after the sun has set.

Crocodile basking open-mouthed on a river bank

Feeding

All crocodilians are carnivores (meat eaters), but they cannot chew their food. Their long jaws and strong, sharp teeth are made for seizing prey and for biting and ripping off pieces they can swallow. A crocodilian opens its mouth by raising its head and allowing the lower jaw to drop open. The muscles for opening the jaws are weak, but the muscles for closing the jaws, and keeping them closed, are very strong.

Crocodilians do not always eat every day. The time between feedings often depends on how large the last meal was or how often food is available. A large crocodilian can survive on a surprisingly small amount of food. This is because it does not burn up much food as fuel to keep itself warm, and it leads a relatively inactive life.

◀ Crocodile feeding on a magpie goose

▼ New teeth form in the hollow centers of a crocodilian's teeth. Old and worn teeth are continually replaced or shed as the new teeth grow and push the old ones out of their sockets from below.

Nesting

After mating, the female crocodile makes a nest in which she lays white, oval, hard-shelled eggs. Nests are either large mounds of mud and grasses that the female scratches together with her front feet, or holes dug in sand or mud. The female makes sure her eggs are well covered.

Nests are always close to water so the hatchlings can reach the water quickly to escape enemies such as birds, large lizards, snakes, and furred animals.

Female crocodile guarding her nesting mound

INSIDE THE EGG

This diagram shows an egg with parts of the shell and inner membranes peeled away to show the developing baby alligator—the *embryo*

The embryo in the diagram is about half-way through its development. This is an alligator's egg, but all crocodilians develop in much the same way

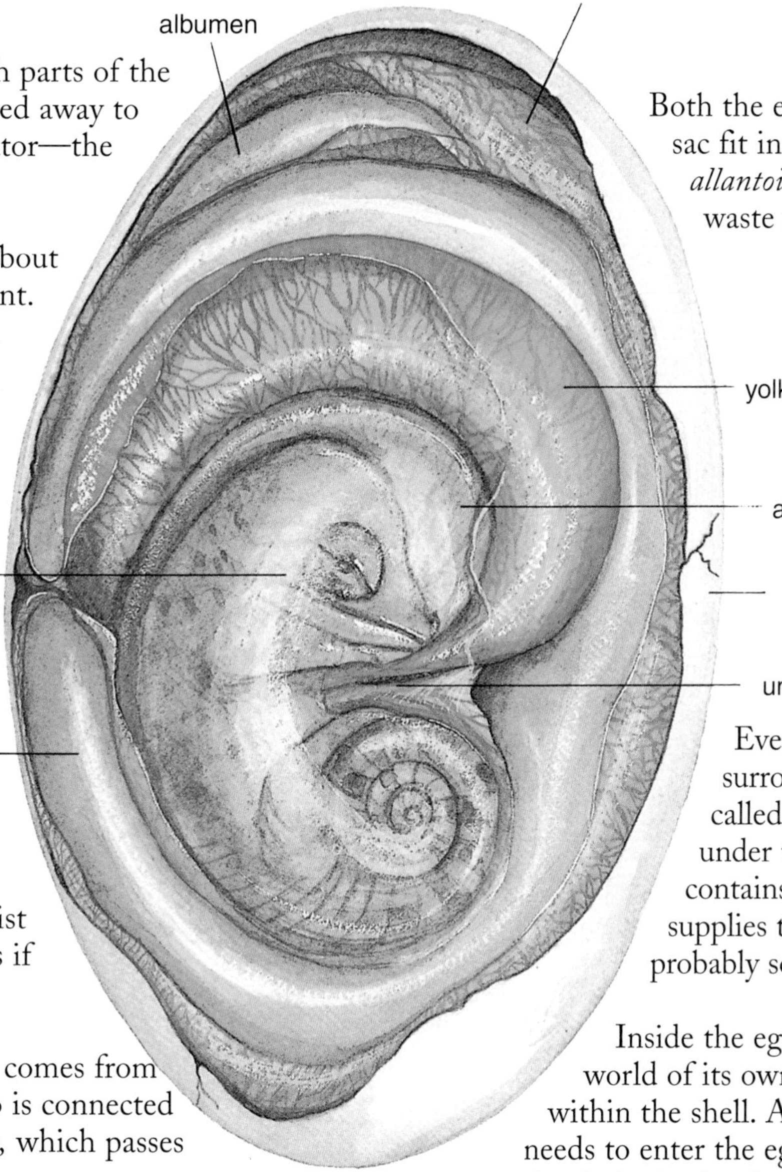

albumen

chorion

Both the egg yolk and the amniotic sac fit inside another sac called the *allantois*, which stores the embryo's waste materials

yolk

amniotic sac

shell

embryo

umbilical stalk

allantois

Everything inside the egg is surrounded by a tough membrane called the *chorion*, which is just under the shell. The chorion contains *albumen* (egg white). It supplies the embryo with water, and probably some food

The embryo is inside a fluid-filled sac called the *amniotic sac*. The fluid keeps the embryo moist and helps protect it from bumps if the nest is disturbed

The embryo's main food supply comes from the yolk of the egg. The embryo is connected to the yolk by the *umbilical stalk*, which passes through the amniotic sac

Inside the egg, the embryo lives in a small world of its own. Everything it needs is within the shell. Air is the only substance that needs to enter the egg, which it does through tiny holes in the shell

Hatching

Crocodilian eggs take about 12 to 14 weeks to hatch. At hatching time, movements in the egg cause the membrane under the shell to bulge. The baby crocodilian then rips the membrane with a sharp egg tooth, which grows at the tip of its snout, and struggles from its broken egg shell. The egg tooth drops off a few days later.

A crocodilian "creche"

A female crocodilian is never far from her nest at hatching time. As soon as the female hears the babies calling and yelping inside their eggs, she scratches the sand or mud and grass litter from the top of the nest with her front feet and sets the brood free. She may also break open the eggs with her jaws.

The mother crocodilian protects her hatchlings from predators as they scurry down to the water and gather around her. Sometimes the mother may carry the babies gently to the water. A group of hatchlings guarded by their mother is called a *creche,* or pod.

The hatchlings have to find their own food immediately. They snap up insects, spiders, tadpoles, frogs—whatever tiny creatures in their environment are small enough for them to eat. However, if suitable food is scarce, a young crocodilian can survive for many weeks on the remains of the rich yolk sac it absorbed before breaking out of its egg.

The mother guards the young crocodilians in the creche for several weeks, but no matter how vigilant she is, many of them are eaten by water birds, reptiles, and other animals.

THE THREE TYPES OF CROCODILIANS

There are three types of crocodilians—crocodiles, alligators (including caimans), and gharials.

Most crocodiles have narrow snouts, but a few species have short, wide snouts. The fourth tooth on the lower jaw of all species of crocodiles shows clearly when the jaws are closed.

An alligator's snout is broader than a crocodile's and the tip is more rounded. When an alligator's jaws are closed, the fourth tooth on the lower jaw fits into a socket in the upper jaw so the tooth is hidden from sight. This is an easy way to tell an alligator from a crocodile.

A gharial has a long, very narrow snout.

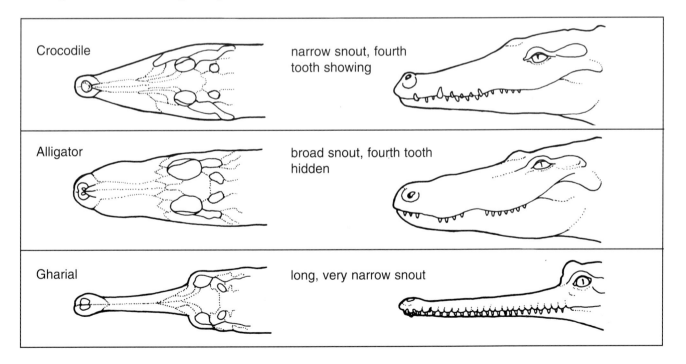

**Existing crocodilian species
in the three groups**

Alligators (Alligatoridae)

American alligator
Chinese alligator
Spectacled caiman
Yacare caiman
Broad-nosed caiman
Black caiman
Cuvier's dwarf caiman
Schneider's smooth-fronted
  caiman

Crocodiles (Crocodilidae)

American crocodile
African slender-snouted crocodile
Orinoco crocodile
Australian freshwater crocodile
Philippines crocodile
Morelet's crocodile
Nile crocodile
New Guinea crocodile
Mugger or marsh crocodile
Saltwater or estuarine crocodile
Cuban crocodile
Siamese crocodile
African dwarf crocodile

Gharials (Gavialidae)

False gharial or Malayan gharial
Gharial

CROCODILIANS—WORLD DISTRIBUTION

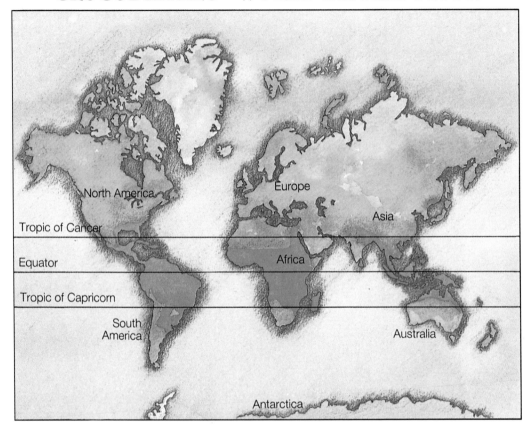

**Areas where crocodilians are found are shown in green. Crocodilians are in all the
tropical and sub-tropical regions of the world.**

Note:

Not all the crocodilians listed here are considered distinct species by all scientists.
Many scientists believe that some species are so closely related they should be
called subspecies.

C R O C O D I L E S

True crocodiles are found throughout Southeast Asia, India, many of the Pacific Islands, northern Australia, Papua New Guinea, the Philippine Islands, tropical Africa and Madagascar, central and northern South America, some of the Caribbean Islands, Cuba, and the southern tip of Florida.

Although Australia does not have any alligators, three Australian rivers are called the West, South, and East Alligator Rivers. These rivers were named in the early 1800s by Captain Phillip Parker King who, while exploring parts of the northern Australian coast, came across what he thought were alligators swimming in estuaries. It is now known that Captain King saw crocodiles, not alligators, but the names of the rivers have never been changed.

In Australia, estuarine crocodiles are also called saltwater crocodiles. They are sea-going crocodiles, and they can swim long distances around the coasts and across the sea.

Distribution map for saltwater crocodiles in Asia and Australia

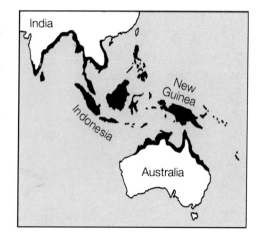

Crocodiles prefer to live in tropical, heavily vegetated rivers, lakes, mangroves, and swamps.

Habitat

Some crocodiles live in the wide, saltwater mouths of tropical rivers where mangrove trees grow close together in the river mud and tall grasses cover the banks. Other crocodiles are found further up the rivers in freshwater. There, mangroves share the banks with tall river eucalyptus trees and enormous clumps of reeds, and water lilies grow in the lagoons and marshes of the vast freshwater wetlands. Crocodiles can often be seen basking open-mouthed in the sun on the banks of these rivers and lagoons.

In tropical Australia, the weather is hot and dry from about April to October. For the remaining months, roughly November to March, it is hot and very wet. During the wet season, torrential rains sweep across the land and the rivers rise and overflow their banks.

Both saltwater and freshwater crocodiles thrive in these warm, wet, marshy conditions. While saltwater crocodiles live in coastal areas, freshwater crocodiles tend to live in inland wetlands and rivers.

Appearance

Its large jaws, powerful body and massive tail make a fully grown crocodile an impressive sight. Some male crocodiles, like the saltwater American and Nile crocodiles, grow to about 20 feet (6 meters) measured from the tip of the snout to the end of the tail.

The greatest age a crocodile can reach is not known, but it is certain that many live for over 70 years.

A saltwater crocodile with yellow-brown hide, splotched with black

▲ **The slide marks on the river bank were made by a crocodile hurrying to the water.**

▶ **Saltwater crocodile feeding on a water bird**

Moving around

A crocodile on land can move amazingly fast for short distances, such as when charging from the water to seize prey on a bank. Using its sharp claws, the crocodile can climb up muddy or sandy river banks. When in a hurry to reach the water, it will often slide on its belly down a sloping, muddy bank. A large crocodile cannot walk very far without resting, but during the wet season some travel quite long distances from one river or marshy place to another, resting along the way.

Feeding

A large crocodile can survive for over a year without eating at all.

When swimming in the sea, saltwater crocodiles feed mainly on fish, but they also eat turtles and sea snakes.

In rivers and lagoons, crocodiles have a wider choice of food. As well as fish, they may capture birds, small mammals, wild pigs, water buffalo, cattle, lizards, snakes, and smaller crocodiles. Crocodiles may launch themselves from the water to grab a low-flying bird, or they may seize a lizard or monkey on an overhanging branch.

In fact, crocodiles may attack any creature swimming in or near the water. They will also attack any animal that comes to the water to drink or that walks close to the water's edge, provided the animal is not too large for the crocodile to grab and haul into the water to drown. Only a very large crocodile will attack a fully-grown buffalo, although calves are often taken.

Crocodiles will often lie in wait for an animal that uses the same drinking spot time after time. If the animal comes to drink when the crocodile is hungry, it floats silently and almost invisibly towards its victim. Suddenly the crocodile will rush out of the water and its jaws will close on the victim's muzzle or leg. Then the crocodile rolls over completely, throwing the victim off its feet. Sometimes the victim may be knocked to the ground by a sweep of the crocodile's powerful tail before being grabbed. No matter which method of overcoming its prey the crocodile uses, the struggling animal is dragged into the water and held under the surface until it drowns. The crocodile then tears pieces of meat from the carcass and swallows them. Small creatures, such as fish, crabs, small mammals, and some small birds, are swallowed whole.

Large pebbles are often found in the stomachs of crocodiles and other crocodilians. Some scientists think these pebbles help grind the crocodilians' food into pieces that are small enough to be easily digested. Other scientists believe that crocodilians scoop up the

Well hidden among the water plants, a saltwater crocodile waits for prey.

pebbles accidentally when they are seizing prey on the bed of a river or lagoon. Still others believe the pebbles are swallowed to act as ballast, helping the crocodilians keep their balance in water. No one really knows for sure.

Mating

Most crocodiles mate during the wet season. Mating occurs wherever the banks of rivers and lagoons are suitable for nesting, and they always mate in shallow water. Males and females locate one another with growling and hissing noises and a musky-smelling scent given off from glands under their throats. During the mating season the male crocodile chooses a territory, and he will fight any other male that enters it. The males roar loudly as they fight. They often suffer serious injuries, such as the loss of a leg, and sometimes they fight to the death.

Nesting

The female crocodile chooses a spot for her nest among tall grasses and bushes on a firm bank. Using her strong hind legs, she scrapes grass, leaf-litter, and mud into a mound. She lays between 40 and 80 eggs on the mound and then covers them with more vegetation and mud. A completed nesting mound measures about 6½ feet (2 meters) across and almost 3¼ feet (1 meter) in height.

Female saltwater crocodile guarding her nesting mound

Unfortunately, some rivers are so subject to heavy flooding that many nests are flooded and the eggs drown before they hatch. Some crocodiles, like the Nile crocodile, dig a hole in a sandy river bank or sandbar and lay their eggs there. The heat of the sun hatches the eggs.

Whether the outside of the nesting mound is wet after rain or baked hard during periods of sunshine, the cavity containing the eggs is always moist. As the vegetation inside the mound decays, it gives off heat and incubates the eggs. Saltwater crocodile eggs must have temperatures between 80.6°F (27°C) and 91.4°F (33°C) to hatch. Many eggs are lost because the nest is too hot or too cold.

The central area at the top of the nest is the warmest. The bottom and towards the edges are cooler. The temperature at which an egg is incubated determines the sex of the developing embryo. Extra high nest temperatures produce males. Low nest temperatures produce females.

The female crocodile digs a wallow in the mud close to her nesting mound. There she lies, almost covered with water or mud, watching her nest to protect the eggs from predators. Occasionally she will lie on top of the mound. If a predator discovers the nest and begins to raid it, the mother roars loudly and charges from her wallow in a fury. After the intruder has been chased away or killed, the mother repairs the nest so the eggs that have not been damaged will have a chance to hatch.

Evidence gathered by scientists suggests that the female does not feed often during the three month incubation period. She lives on fat stored in her body.

At hatching time, the hatchlings call to their mother as they struggle to break through their eggshells. This alerts the mother to scratch open the nesting mound. The hatchlings would smother if she did not help them get out of the mound fairly quickly. Sometimes the mother will

Female crocodile in a mud wallow

gently pick up an egg in her large jaws and carefully crack the shell with her teeth to help a hatchling emerge. Newly-hatched crocodiles are about 10 to 12 inches (250 to 300 millimeters) long.

The mother crocodile guards her hatchlings from predators, including other crocodiles, as they hurry to the water. She continues to watch over the creche for several weeks.

At first the hatchlings eat insects, spiders, tiny crabs, freshwater crayfish, and other small water creatures. As the hatchlings grow and their swimming skills improve, they learn to grab fish.

Crocodiles hatching. On the left, only the snout of the hatchling breaking out of the egg can be seen.

Creche, or pod, of crocodiles in a crocodile "nursery" pool where the mother crocodile lives with her babies

Surviving

When young crocodiles grow to about 3¼ feet (1 meter) or more in length, older, larger crocodiles usually force them to leave the river where they were reared. The older crocodiles see the river as their own territory.

Many young crocodiles that are forced down river are taken by predators or larger crocodiles. If there are creeks or swamps near the river, young crocodiles are sometimes able to hide there until they have grown larger.

Some scientists think displaced crocodiles that have survived and

grown may return to the river in which they were bred and try to establish territories of their own. To do so they would have to fight older crocodiles, who always guard their territories fiercely. A crocodile that has reached maturity is a real survivor. Not many hatchlings live that long.

Caution

In many tropical areas there are signs warning of the danger of crocodiles. Yet many tourists, and even people who live in these areas, ignore the signs. Although people may not actually swim in a river, or camp on the bank, they often fish, walk, or take their dogs for a run quite close to the water's edge. To the crocodile, people, pet dogs, and its usual prey are all flesh, and flesh is food. Unwary people and pets have been seized by large crocodiles.

▲ This sign warns swimmers of crocodiles in Australia.

▼ Distribution map for Australian freshwater crocodiles

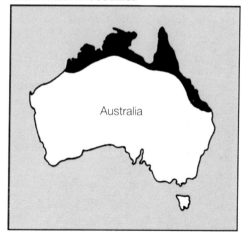

FRESHWATER CROCODILES

The freshwater crocodiles of Australia are also known as Johnston's, fish crocodiles, river crocodiles, and "freshies." Robert Arthur Johnston, a sub-inspector of police in North Queensland, Australia, in the 1800s, was the first white person to report the existence of large numbers of crocodiles in the freshwater stretches of some northern rivers. Actually, there are more than 11 species of crocodiles that live in tropical freshwater habitats throughout the world.

Habitat

Freshwater crocodiles are usually found away from the coast in the rivers, creeks, and lagoons of tropical regions, but some are able to live in quite salty water. Crocodiles and alligators have salt glands on their tongues to get rid of excess salt in their bodies. However, not many freshwater crocodiles live in the saltwater river mouths because the larger and more aggressive crocodiles chase them away or kill them.

Freshwater crocodile basking on a rocky outcrop near a lagoon in northern Australia

Appearance

Freshwater crocodiles vary in size. They may be small like the African dwarf crocodile, slender like the Malayan false gharial, or massive like the saltwater crocodile. The snouts of some crocodiles are long and narrow and highly specialized.

Feeding

The crocodile's narrow snout sweeps easily through the water as it snatches fish, its main food. These crocodiles also eat spiders, insects, tadpoles, frogs, turtles, freshwater crayfish, small lizards, and water rats. Sometimes they may eat small birds, snatching the birds from the air as they dip to the surface of the water to drink. Freshwater crocodiles will even eat smaller crocodiles of their own kind.

The body of the freshwater crocodile is more streamlined than the saltwater crocodile's.

Mating

Freshwater crocodiles mate in water. The males and females locate one another with loud growling and hissing noises and a musky scent given off from their scent glands.

Nesting

Freshwater crocodiles nest between August and September, during tropical Australia's dry season. The female makes a nest for her eggs by scooping a hollow in a sandy bank close to the water. She lays from 12 to 24 eggs which she then covers with sand.

Female freshwater crocodiles have not often been seen protecting their nests from intruders. Unprotected eggs are taken by wild pigs, goannas, and other predators. Most eggs have hatched before the wet season begins, so not many are destroyed by floods.

Freshwater crocodiles take about 3 months to hatch. At hatching time the sounds made by the young crocodiles attract the mother. She then accompanies the hatchlings to the water where they gather around her for protection. However, large numbers of freshwater hatchlings are lost. Towards the end of the dry season many lagoons shrink or dry up altogether. Without the shelter of the shallow waters, the hatchlings become easy prey for larger crocodiles and other

Resting in a dry rock hole puts the freshwater hatchling at risk of being caught by a predator.

predators. Scientists estimate that 9 out of every 10 hatchlings die before they are a year old.

Caution

Crocodiles are shy creatures. Most are harmless to people unless they are interfered with or accidentally trodden on. Some of the larger species are dangerous and they may sometimes attack people and pets. Mother crocodiles protect their young and may attack people when baby crocodiles or nests are molested. Crocodiles should never be touched. Even hatchlings will bite and scratch furiously to defend themselves. In many countries, it is illegal to interfere with any crocodile.

Freshwater crocodile "galloping" across dry ground, heading for the safety of a nearby lagoon. It has probably been disturbed by humans. Crocodiles can go as fast as 12 ½ miles (20 kilometers) per hour.

ALLIGATORS

At a glance, alligators and crocodiles look very much alike, but there are some important differences in both appearance and behavior between these two kinds of crocodilians. There are also differences in the climate of their habitats.

Members of the alligator family are found in the southeastern United States, Central and South America, and China. True alligators are found only in the United States and China.

Habitat

The habitat of the American alligator is the southeastern area of the United States where summers can be very warm but winters are often cold. The American alligator lives in fresh or brackish water.

Alligators were once common in the rivers, lakes, and marshes around the Gulf of Mexico as far south as Florida. They were also found as far north as North Carolina. Over the past century, much of their natural habitat has been destroyed. Large areas of wetlands have been drained for farming. These days alligators are found mostly in the coastal wetlands of Louisiana and Florida.

Distribution map for American alligators

United States of America

In the Everglades of Florida, pines, palms, and lacy cypress trees merge with thick mangrove swamps. Clumps of trees and shrubs form on "tree islands" in the marshes. In some places, saw grass grows nearly 13 feet (4 meters) high. In other places, the surface of the water is covered with water lilies and other aquatic vegetation.

Examples of the habitat of the American alligator in Florida
◀**Water Lettuce Lake, Corkscrew Swamp**
▲**Lake Alice**

To keep from freezing during cold weather, American alligators dig dens in which they spend the winter months protected from the cold.

An alligator's den is usually at or below water level. The den has a narrow entrance, but at the other end the alligator has enough room to turn around and face the opening. On sunny winter days, alligators come out of their dens and lie on the river banks basking in the sunshine. This, too, helps them keep warm.

Occasionally there may be an extremely cold winter and not all alligators are able to survive, even in their dens. For example, in 1981, exceptionally cold weather killed large numbers of alligators because their bodies were not able to cope with the extremely low temperatures.

American alligator on a log in the Florida swamps

Appearance

The American alligator does not reach the length of a fully-grown saltwater crocodile, but it is more heavily built. The adult alligator's hide is dark gray or black.

The alligator's snout is broader and more rounded at the tip than a crocodile's, and the fourth tooth on an alligator's lower jaw is hidden when its jaws are closed.

Moving around

On land, the American alligator can charge with speed, but in general, it is not as aggressive as some crocodiles. In water, the alligator can match a crocodile's torpedo-like swiftness and agility when changing course, turning, or leaping partly out of the water to seize prey.

Feeding

The American alligator feeds on fish and other water creatures such as crayfish, shrimp, crabs, frogs, and turtles. Alligators also eat snakes, lizards, birds, and small mammals, such as nutria, muskrats, and raccoons, that are native to the swamplands. Sometimes they may even eat deer.

When an alligator is swimming, it often catches food that is too big to be swallowed whole. Then it raises its head above the water, as it always does when swallowing, and crushes the food, sometimes snapping it in two with a sidewards jerk of its head.

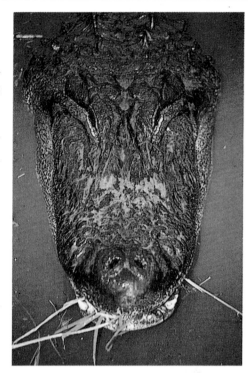

View of an American alligator's head showing its broad snout, which is rounded at the tip

American alligator crushing a water bird in its jaws

An alligator does not eat during the winter months because its body is not warm enough to digest food properly. It lives on fat stored in its body.

Mating

Alligators mate in water. They make bellowing noises when attracting mates. The mating season for American alligators is May to June (late spring to early summer).

Nesting

The female alligator nests three to four weeks after mating. Like many crocodiles, the alligator scratches together a mound of mud and vegetation. In the center she lays between 30 and 50 eggs which she then covers with more nesting materials. The completed mound measures about 6½ feet (2 meters) across and just under 3¼ feet (1 meter) in height. Heat from the sun plus heat given off by decaying vegetation in the nest keeps the temperature inside the mound between 75.2°F (24°C) and 91.4°F (33°C).

Female American alligator guarding her nesting mound

The female alligator stays close to her nest during the eight weeks it takes for the eggs to hatch. During these weeks she guards the nest fiercely from predators, such as raccoons, who often destroy a nest to eat the eggs.

When the mother alligator hears the grunting noises made by the baby alligators at hatching time she pulls the nest apart with her front feet to set them free.

Some hatchlings have more trouble breaking through their shells than others. Mother alligators, like mother crocodiles, have been known to crack an egg between their teeth to help a hatchling emerge. Mother alligators, like some mother crocodiles, will also sometimes pick up their newly-hatched young in their mouths and carry them to the water. And like the mother crocodile, the mother alligator protects her young in a creche for the first months of their lives.

Young alligators are about 8 inches (230 millimeters) long when they hatch. Their bodies are banded in yellow and black, but the stripes fade as the alligators grow. Like crocodile hatchlings, baby alligators must find their own food as soon as they enter the water. They eat insects, spiders, and any small water creatures that come along. Young alligators often fall prey to large fish, snakes, water birds, foxes, raccoons, and other animals.

GHARIALS

Gharials are also known as gavials. They are large, mainly fish-eating crocodilians with extremely long, slender snouts.

Habitat

Gharials prefer fast-flowing clear water with deep pools. They dig their nests in sandy banks and sandbars and bask in the sun to keep warm during the winter months. The rivers that flow through India, Pakistan, Nepal, Bangladesh, Bhutan, and Burma were the original habitat of gharials.

Years ago there were large numbers of gharials in rivers such as the Indus, the Ganges, and the Brahmaputra, but today this crocodilian is an endangered species. In the Chambal River in western India, a gharial sanctuary has been established. The gharial is thought to be already extinct in Burma and Bhutan.

Distribution map for gharials

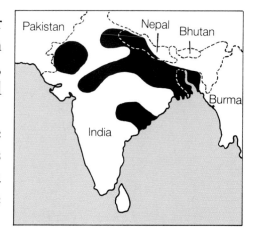

Appearance

A gharial may grow to nearly 21 feet (7 meters) in length. The hide of its long body is olive green on the upper surface and pale yellow on the underparts. It has over 100 fine, pointed teeth in its long, extremely narrow jaws.

Gharials on a rock ledge. The deep, clear pool behind them is typical of their habitat.

Feeding

With a sudden sideways sweep of its long, slender jaws, a gharial seizes a fish across its middle. The gharial then raises its snout above water and the fish is juggled around so that it can be swallowed head first. In this way, the fins and gills flatten against the fish's body and do not catch in the gharial's throat.

At times gharials capture birds, and they have also been known to seize goats and dogs at the water's edge. Attacks on humans are extremely rare, so gharials have never been feared.

Gharial feeding on fish

Head of a male gharial showing the hollow, bony knob at the tip of its snout

Mating

Gharials mate in the water. The male may approach several females before one accepts him. Hissing and snorting sounds are made by both the male and female. The male can make very loud sounds, almost like a steam train. These noises are amplified by the hollow, bony knob that many large, older male gharials have surrounding their nostrils.

Nesting

The nesting season of the gharial is from late March to mid-April. After mating, the female gharial digs several trial nests. These are dug in sand banks either at the river's edge or midstream. Then she digs her true nest in which she lays her eggs. Digging is arduous for gharials because their legs are shorter than those of crocodiles and alligators, and their movements on land are slow.

A gharial's nest must have just the right balance of sand and moisture and be sufficiently deep for the temperature inside to remain between 89.6°F (32°C) and 93.2°F (34°C). A gharial lays between 25 and 60 eggs. They take from 12 to 13 weeks to incubate.

The female gharial guards her nest, helps her young escape from the nest at hatching time, and looks after them in a creche for several months.

Many animals prey on young gharials. Eggs and hatchlings are seized by fish, monitor lizards, birds of prey, and jackals. Floods are another danger. Whole nests can be destroyed when a river rises.

CONSERVATION OF CROCODILIANS

Crocodilians have survived for 190 million years, but today there is a possibility that many species may become extinct.

Some people believe an animal should be killed if it endangers the humans who have moved into the animal's natural habitat. People also kill animals in the wild because the hides, fur, or some other parts or by-products can be sold for a great deal of money. For example, elephants are killed by poachers for their ivory tusks and rhinoceroses are killed for their horns. Today, crocodilians in the wild are sometimes killed out of fear, but more often for their hides. The smooth belly skin is used to make articles of clothing such as shoes, wallets, belts, and handbags.

Commercial skin hunting brought most species of crocodilians to the brink of extinction as populations were seriously depleted during the early and mid 1900s.

The bag on the right is made of crocodile skin. The bag behind it is made of imitation crocodile skin. Modern processes make it hard to tell the difference between the two, but the genuine crocodile skin bag is much more expensive.

CROCODILES

Some scientists believe that before the 1940s there were about 1,000,000 saltwater crocodiles in Australia. They estimate that from 1945 to 1972, about 300,000 of these crocodiles were shot for their skins, which brought high prices in Australia and around the world.

Even very young crocodiles, especially freshwater crocodiles, were not safe from the hunters. They were caught, killed, stuffed, and then mounted so they looked alive. Tourists bought them as "stuffies," the local name for stuffed crocodiles.

By 1970, most of the crocodile hunters were gone from the north of Australia. So were many of the crocodiles.

▼A 1952 letter from some crocodile hunters in northern Australia to friends in Melbourne

Jack has an order for 50 small 'freshies' at five pounds, ten shillings each. They will be stuffed and sold to tourists as mementos. We are going out to catch the crocs today. We are going on another hunt to shoot large saltwater crocs on Wednesday. We'll be gone for two days and expect to get a good haul in that time.

▶An old photograph of crocodile hunters in northern Australia during the 1920s

Protection by law

Since the early 1970s, crocodiles and alligators have been regulated by law. Some critically endangered species are protected and are not allowed to be hunted and killed. However, many regions where crocodiles live are remote, vast, wild areas. It is difficult for wildlife officers and police to patrol these areas and enforce the protection laws. Poachers in many countries continue to kill crocodilians for their hides.

Crocodiles are also killed accidentally. Each year many crocodiles in Australia become entangled in strong nets that are secured in the rivers to catch fish. Crocodiles caught in these nets drown because they are trapped underwater for too long. Others are killed because people fear them.

Officers of the Australian Northern Territory Conservation Commission measuring a large male saltwater crocodile. The crocodile was trapped in a heavy rope net and removed from the popular fishing area it inhabited.

When a large crocodile becomes a danger to people in settled areas it is often trapped by wildlife officers and killed.

Crocodile farms

Crocodile farms have recently been established in a number of countries. On production farms, crocodiles are bred and raised for their hides and meat. Teeth and claws are sold to tourists as souvenirs. Other farms cater mainly to tourists. Visitors are protected by security fences and can view the crocodiles at close range.

Crocodile farm

Conservation of habitat

Crocodiles in many tropical regions are at risk of becoming extinct through human encroachment, land development, and habitat loss. If large areas of the marshy wetlands are drained to provide land for new houses and the development of industries, much of the habitat of the world's crocodilians will be destroyed, endangering their survival.

It is estimated that from a combination of legal harvesting and illegal poaching 2,000,000 crocodilians are killed each year throughout the world for their skins.

ALLIGATORS

From the late 1800s until well into the 1960s, the American alligator was hunted for sport and for its hide. By 1967, the alligator had become so scarce it was classified as an endangered species and protected by law.

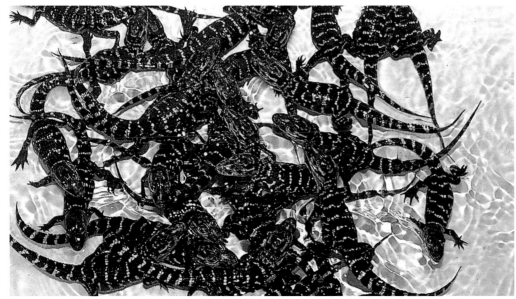

Pod of two-day-old American alligator hatchlings at an alligator farm

Members of a conservation program in the Royal Chitwan National Park in Nepal release a gharial bred in captivity. About 200 have been released up to now. By fitting the gharials with radio transmitter collars, researchers have found that about 30 percent of these gharials survive.

In the following 10 years the number of alligators increased so much that the species was reclassified as a threatened species. This meant a limited number of people could buy licenses allowing them to shoot alligators for their hides.

In the United States, alligators have been farmed since the 1930s, and alligator farming is now a large industry.

GHARIALS

In the past, gharials were hunted for sport and for their skins, and thousands were killed. In some areas, villagers have traditionally gathered gharial eggs for food. More recently, large dams have been built across rivers inhabited by gharials and their nesting banks are now covered by water. Many gharials have drowned when they were caught in large nylon fishing nets. Gharials are now an endangered species.

In the 1970s, special sanctuaries for these ancient reptiles were established in India, Nepal, and Pakistan. Gharials are also now protected by law in India, Nepal, Bangladesh, and Pakistan, and commercial net-fishing is banned in all gharial sanctuaries.

People everywhere should realize the urgent need to protect all the animals that share our world and the special habitats in which they live. We must find a balance between our needs and those of the animals. Otherwise, many more of them will become extinct.

GLOSSARY

ballast   material carried (usually by ships) to give balance and stability

carnivore   animal that eats meat

cold-blooded   body temperature dependent upon the temperature of the surroundings

creche   nursery

embryo   animal in the early stages of development, before it has hatched or been born

estuarine   of, or living in, an estuary

estuary   wide tidal mouth of a river

evaporate   to change from a liquid to a vapor or gas

extinct   no longer existing; having died out

fossil   remains or impression of a plant or an animal hardened and preserved in the Earth's layers

gland   organ or group of cells that produce chemicals used by the body

incubate   to provide heat to promote the development of an embryo in an egg

lagoon   shallow body of water that is usually connected to the sea

membrane   thin layer of animal or plant tissue

predator   animal that hunts and kills other animals

prey   animal hunted or killed by another animal for food

species   distinct group of animals or plants that interbreed and have many features in common

territory   defined area; the area claimed and defended by an animal or animal pair

tropical   very hot and humid

tropics   area of the Earth's surface between the Tropic of Cancer and the Tropic of Capricorn

warm-blooded   capable of regulating its own body temperature

webbing   tissue that creates a web; joined by a web

wetland   very moist area such as a marsh or swamp

INDEX

Note: Page numbers in italics refer to photographs or illustrations.